AF417060

Manifest in Minutes

Manifest in Minutes

Matthew Petchinsky

Manifest in Minutes: The Quick Law of Attraction Guide
By: Matthew Petchinsky

Introduction

The Law of Attraction is a profound and transformative principle that has captured the attention of millions worldwide, promising the ability to shape reality through the power of thoughts, emotions, and intentions. At its core, the Law of Attraction is rooted in the belief that like attracts like, meaning that the energy we emit through our thoughts and feelings has a direct impact on the experiences and outcomes we encounter in life. This universal principle empowers individuals to take control of their lives by aligning their mindset with their desires, ultimately opening the door to a life of abundance, happiness, and fulfillment.

In our fast-paced world, the challenge for many lies not in understanding the Law of Attraction but in finding the time and focus to apply it effectively. With countless responsibilities and distractions vying for our attention, it can be easy to dismiss the power of manifestation as something unattainable or time-consuming. However, the truth is that meaningful change does not require hours of meditation or elaborate rituals. Instead, quick, focused actions can yield powerful, life-changing results. When approached with clarity and intention, even small moments of alignment can spark profound transformations.

This book is designed to bridge the gap between understanding and action, offering a practical and time-efficient approach to manifestation. Whether you are new to the Law of Attraction or seeking to refine your practice, this guide will equip you with actionable steps that fit seamlessly into your busy schedule. By breaking down the process into manageable techniques, you will discover how to harness the power of your thoughts and emotions in as little as a few minutes a day.

Throughout these chapters, you will find exercises, affirmations, and strategies tailored to help you identify your desires, shift your mindset, and align your energy with your goals. Each method has been carefully curated to maximize results without overwhelming your daily routine. From cultivating gratitude to visualizing your dreams with laser-sharp focus, this book provides a roadmap for manifesting your ideal reality with efficiency and confidence.

The journey of transformation begins here. Together, we will explore the profound potential of the Law of Attraction and uncover the tools needed to bring your dreams to life. Remember, manifestation is not about waiting for the perfect moment or ideal conditions—it's about taking inspired action right now. With this guide in hand, you hold the key to unlocking the life you've always envisioned. The only question is, are you ready to begin?

Chapter 1: The Foundations of Manifestation

Manifestation begins with understanding the foundational principles that govern the Law of Attraction—a universal law that states that like attracts like. At its essence, this law asserts that the energy we emit, through our thoughts, emotions, and beliefs, determines the reality we experience. By mastering the core principles of energy, vibration, and alignment, we can actively shape our lives and bring our deepest desires into fruition.

The Core Principles of the Law of Attraction

1. Energy

   Everything in the universe, including ourselves, is made of energy. This energy is in constant motion, forming the fabric of our reality. Our thoughts and emotions are energetic forces, radiating frequencies that interact with the world around us. Positive, high-frequency energy, such as joy, gratitude, and love, attracts positive outcomes, while negative, low-frequency energy, such as fear, doubt, and resentment, draws undesirable experiences. Understanding this principle is crucial because it means we hold the power to influence what we attract into our lives simply by shifting our energy.

2. Vibration

   Vibration is the specific frequency at which our energy resonates. Think of it as the "tuning fork" of your personal reality. When you consistently vibrate at a high frequency by focusing on positive emotions and beliefs, you align yourself with desirable outcomes. Conversely, a low-frequency vibration, often driven by negative beliefs or unresolved fears, misaligns you with your goals. The key is learning to consciously elevate your vibration through practices like gratitude, visualization, and mindfulness.

3. **Alignment**

   Alignment is the harmonious relationship between your desires, thoughts, beliefs, and actions. It occurs when your internal world (thoughts and emotions) and external world (actions and behaviors) are congruent with what you wish to manifest. For example, if you desire financial abundance but harbor beliefs of scarcity or engage in habits of over-spending, you are out of alignment. True alignment requires that your energy matches the vibration of your desired outcome, creating a clear pathway for manifestation.

How Beliefs and Thoughts Shape Reality

Our beliefs and thoughts act as the blueprint for our reality. What we believe to be true influences how we perceive the world, the choices we make, and ultimately, the outcomes we experience. For example, a person who believes they are unworthy of love may unconsciously sabotage relationships, reinforcing that belief. Conversely, someone who believes they are deserving of success is more likely to take bold, inspired actions that lead to achievement.

The subconscious mind plays a significant role in this process. While we may consciously desire a specific outcome, subconscious limiting beliefs—those ingrained narratives we've internalized from past experiences, societal conditioning, or fears—can act as invisible barriers to manifestation. Recognizing and shifting these beliefs is a vital step in aligning with your desires.

Exercise: Identifying and Shifting Limiting Beliefs

This simple yet powerful exercise will help you uncover the hidden beliefs that may be blocking your manifestation efforts and guide you in transforming them.

1. Step 1: Identify a Desire

   Choose one specific goal or desire you wish to manifest, such as improving your financial situation, finding love, or achieving career success. Write it down in a clear, concise statement. For example, "I want to earn $10,000 per month doing work I love."

2. Step 2: Explore Your Beliefs

   Reflect on the desire you've written and ask yourself:
   - What thoughts come to mind when I think about achieving this goal?
   - Do I feel excitement or doubt?
   - Are there any fears or "what if" scenarios that arise?

Write down all the beliefs or feelings that surface, both positive and negative. For example:

-
  - Positive belief: "I have valuable skills that people will pay for."
  - Limiting belief: "I'm not experienced enough to make that much money."

1. Step 3: Challenge Limiting Beliefs

   For each limiting belief, ask yourself:
   - Is this belief absolutely true?
   - Where did this belief come from?
   - What evidence do I have to support or contradict it?

Often, you'll find that limiting beliefs are based on past experiences or assumptions rather than objective truths. For example, the belief "I'm not experienced enough" might stem from a single instance of rejection, not a universal truth.

1. Step 4: Rewrite the Narrative
   Transform each limiting belief into a positive, empowering affirmation. For example:
   ◦ Limiting belief: "I'm not experienced enough to make that much money."
   ◦ Affirmation: "Every day, I gain more experience and attract opportunities that value my skills."

Write these affirmations down and repeat them daily, ideally in front of a mirror or during a moment of stillness.

1. Step 5: Align Actions with Beliefs
   Finally, take one small, aligned action that supports your new belief. If your affirmation is "I am deserving of financial abundance," an aligned action might be creating a budget, applying for a new job, or starting a side hustle. These actions reinforce your belief and elevate your vibration, bringing you closer to your desire.

Conclusion

Understanding the foundations of manifestation—energy, vibration, and alignment—is the first step in mastering the Law of Attraction. By recognizing how your beliefs shape your reality and learning to identify and shift limiting beliefs, you begin to take control of your energetic blueprint. Manifestation is not about forcing the universe to comply with your wishes; it is about becoming the kind of person who naturally attracts the life they desire. With this foundation in place, you are ready to explore the practical tools and techniques that will make manifestation an integral, effortless part of your daily life.

Chapter 2: Setting Clear and Powerful Intentions

One of the most critical steps in manifestation is setting clear and powerful intentions. Your intention is the compass that guides the energy of the universe toward your desires. Without clarity and focus, your energy may scatter, making it difficult for your goals to materialize. This chapter will teach you how to create specific, high-energy goals, align emotionally with your desires, and implement quick yet effective intention-setting practices that keep you on the path to success.

The Power of Specific, High-Energy Goals

A vague goal produces vague results. If you simply think, "I want to be happier," the universe doesn't have a clear roadmap to follow. Instead, when you set specific, well-defined goals, you send a clear signal about what you want. For example, "I want to wake up every morning feeling grateful, energized, and confident about my day" is a precise intention that defines both the desired state and the emotional experience.

In addition to clarity, high-energy goals amplify your ability to manifest. High-energy goals are those that spark excitement, passion, and a sense of purpose. They should feel inspiring and meaningful to you, not just logical or practical. If a goal doesn't ignite some level of emotional enthusiasm, it's harder to align your energy with it.

Steps to Create Specific, High-Energy Goals:

1. **Be Precise:** Replace broad desires with detailed intentions. For example, instead of "I want more money," specify "I want to earn an extra $1,000 this month through creative and enjoyable work."

2. **Use Positive Language:** Frame your goals in a positive way. Instead of "I don't want to feel stressed anymore," reframe it as "I want to feel calm, focused, and in control of my life."

3. **Make It Personal:** Your goals should resonate deeply with your values and desires, not what others expect of you.

4. **Add a Timeline:** Giving your goal a timeframe adds urgency and focus. For example, "I will secure my dream job within the next three months."

Emotional Alignment with Desires

Setting intentions is not just about thinking or writing down goals—it's about feeling them. Emotional alignment means generating the emotions you would feel if your desire were already fulfilled. This step is crucial because emotions carry a much stronger energetic charge than thoughts alone.

For example, if your goal is to find a loving relationship, imagine the feelings of love, joy, and connection you would experience. By embodying those emotions now, you raise your vibration to match the frequency of your goal, making it easier to attract.

How to Cultivate Emotional Alignment:

1. **Imagine Success:** Close your eyes and visualize your desire as if it has already come true. Focus on how it feels rather than the details of how it happened.
2. **Anchor the Emotion:** Identify a physical gesture or word that represents the feeling, such as placing a hand on your heart or repeating a mantra like "I am worthy of love."
3. **Stay in the Energy:** Throughout your day, revisit that emotional state. Music, movement, or gratitude can help you maintain high-vibrational feelings.

Quick Intention-Setting Practices

Even if you have a busy schedule, these quick practices can help you set and reinforce your intentions effectively. Incorporating them into your routine takes only a few minutes but keeps your energy aligned with your desires.

1. Visualization

Visualization is one of the most powerful tools for intention setting. When you visualize, you create a mental movie of your desired outcome, engaging your senses and emotions to bring it to life.

Steps for Effective Visualization:

- Find a quiet space where you won't be disturbed.
- Close your eyes and take a few deep breaths to relax.
- Picture your goal as if it has already been achieved. Include vivid details: Where are you? Who is with you? What do you see, hear, and feel?
- Focus on the emotions associated with this success—joy, gratitude, pride, or excitement.
- Spend 2-5 minutes immersing yourself in this scene. When done regularly, this practice reprograms your subconscious mind to work toward your goal.

2. Affirmations

Affirmations are positive, empowering statements that reinforce your intentions and help shift your mindset. Repeating affirmations trains your mind to focus on possibilities rather than limitations.

Tips for Creating Powerful Affirmations:

- **Use the Present Tense:** Frame your affirmation as if your goal is already happening. For example, "I am attracting financial abundance every day."
- **Be Positive:** Focus on what you want, not what you want to avoid. Replace "I don't want to struggle with money" with "I am financially secure and thriving."
- **Make It Personal:** Use language that resonates with you and feels authentic.
- **Repeat Often:** Say your affirmations aloud in front of a mirror, write them in a journal, or record and listen to them during quiet moments.

3. Morning Intention Ritual

Start your day with a simple intention-setting ritual to align your energy with your goals.

Steps for a Morning Ritual:

- Before getting out of bed, take a moment to center yourself with deep breathing.
- Think of one goal you want to focus on that day.
- Visualize or say an affirmation about that goal. For example, "Today, I am taking steps toward my dream job with confidence and clarity."
- Express gratitude for the opportunities ahead, even if they haven't appeared yet.

4. Evening Reflection and Reset

End your day with a reflection practice to evaluate your alignment with your intentions.

Steps for Evening Reflection:

- Reflect on what went well and how you aligned with your goals during the day.
- Identify any moments of doubt or misalignment and forgive yourself for them.
- Set a new or revised intention for the following day, focusing on what you want to manifest.

Conclusion

Setting clear and powerful intentions is the foundation of effective manifestation. By creating specific, high-energy goals, aligning emotionally with your desires, and implementing quick intention-setting practices, you establish a strong energetic signal that directs the universe toward your dreams. Remember, the universe responds not just to what you ask for but to the energy and emotion behind it. With clarity, alignment, and consistency, you are well on your way to manifesting the life you envision. Let this chapter serve as a guide to creating the solid, intentional groundwork for all your manifestation efforts to come.

Chapter 3: Visualization in Minutes

Visualization is one of the most powerful tools in the manifestation process. By creating vivid mental images of your goals, you activate the subconscious mind, align your energy with your desires, and accelerate the manifestation process. Even with limited time, you can achieve remarkable results using short, focused visualization practices. In this chapter, we will explore the science behind visualization, provide techniques to create vivid mental images in under five minutes, and share inspiring success stories of manifesting with quick visualization exercises.

The Science Behind Visualization

Visualization works because the mind cannot easily distinguish between a vividly imagined scenario and a real-life experience. This principle, often referred to as mental rehearsal, is supported by neuroscience. When you visualize, your brain activates the same neural pathways as it would if you were physically experiencing the event. This process strengthens the connection between your mind and your goals, making them feel more achievable and natural.

Key aspects of how visualization impacts the subconscious mind include:

1. **Activating the Reticular Activating System (RAS):**
   The RAS is a network of neurons in the brainstem that acts as a filter for sensory information. When you visualize your goals, you program your RAS to prioritize opportunities, resources, and ideas that align with your vision. For example, if you consistently visualize financial success, your RAS will help you notice opportunities that lead to increased income.

2. **Creating Emotional Resonance:**
   Visualization triggers emotions associated with your goals. These emotions raise your vibration and align your energy with your desires. Positive emotions such as joy, gratitude, and excitement create a magnetic force that draws your goals closer.

3. **Reprogramming the Subconscious Mind:**
   The subconscious mind is the seat of deeply held beliefs and habits. By repeatedly visualizing your desired outcomes, you overwrite limiting beliefs and replace them with empowering ones. Over time, your subconscious begins to accept your vision as reality, influencing your actions and decisions in alignment with your goals.

Techniques for Vivid Visualization in Under 5 Minutes

Even the busiest schedules can accommodate these quick and effective visualization practices. Each technique is designed to maximize results in a short amount of time.

1. The Mental Movie Technique

This classic technique involves creating a mental "movie" of your desired outcome.

Steps:

1. Find a quiet space and close your eyes.
2. Take a few deep breaths to relax your mind and body.
3. Picture your goal as a short movie scene. For example, if your goal is to land a dream job, visualize yourself confidently walking into the office, shaking hands with the manager, and receiving the offer letter.
4. Add sensory details. Imagine the sights, sounds, smells, and feelings in the scene.
5. Focus on the emotions of success, such as pride, joy, and gratitude.

Spend 2-5 minutes immersing yourself in this mental movie. Replay it regularly to reinforce the vision.

2. The Snapshot Technique

This technique is perfect for creating quick, impactful visualizations.

Steps:

1. Think of one specific image that represents your goal. For example, if you want financial abundance, the image could be a check for $10,000 with your name on it.
2. Close your eyes and visualize this snapshot in as much detail as possible.
3. Focus on the feelings associated with achieving this goal. Feel excitement, gratitude, and confidence.
4. Hold the image in your mind for 30 seconds to a minute.

This technique is ideal for busy moments when you need a quick boost of focus and alignment.

3. The Vision Board Walkthrough

If you have a vision board, you can use it as a visualization tool.

Steps:

1. Spend a minute or two looking at your vision board, absorbing the images and words you've chosen.
2. Close your eyes and imagine stepping into the scenes on the board. If there's an image of a tropical vacation, picture yourself feeling the sand beneath your feet and hearing the ocean waves.
3. Relive the emotions of achieving these goals, such as joy, peace, or excitement.

This technique combines physical and mental visualization, making it highly effective.

4. The Affirmation Amplifier

Pairing affirmations with visualization amplifies their power.
Steps:

1. Choose an affirmation that aligns with your goal. For example, "I am living my dream life."
2. Close your eyes and visualize a scene that reflects this affirmation. For instance, if your dream life involves a beautiful home, picture yourself walking through its rooms.
3. Repeat the affirmation silently or aloud while holding the visualization in your mind.

This practice takes less than five minutes and reinforces both your mental and verbal intentions.

Success Stories of Quick Visualization Practices

Visualization doesn't require hours of practice to yield significant results. Here are three inspiring stories of people who manifested their dreams using short visualization techniques:

1. Manifesting a Dream Job:

Emma, a recent college graduate, used the Mental Movie Technique to visualize landing her dream job. Each morning, she spent three minutes imagining herself in her ideal role, interacting with colleagues and thriving in her work environment. Within two months, Emma received an offer for a position that perfectly matched her vision.

2. Attracting Financial Abundance:

Carlos, a freelance designer, created a vision board with images of financial prosperity. He practiced the Vision Board Walkthrough technique daily, spending five minutes immersing himself in the feeling of abundance. Within six weeks, Carlos landed several high-paying clients, doubling his income.

3. Reuniting with a Loved One:

Maya wanted to reconnect with her estranged sister. She used the Snapshot Technique to visualize receiving a heartfelt text message from her sister. Maya focused on the emotions of joy and relief while holding this image in her mind. A few days later, she unexpectedly received the exact message she had envisioned.

Conclusion

Visualization is a transformative practice that leverages the power of the mind to shape reality. By understanding the science behind visualization, mastering quick techniques, and drawing inspiration from real-life success stories, you can integrate this powerful tool into your daily life with ease. Remember, it's not the length of time spent visualizing that matters most—it's the clarity, emotion, and consistency you bring to the practice. With just a few minutes a day, you can turn your dreams into tangible realities and take significant steps toward the life you desire.

Chapter 4: Aligning Action with Desire

While setting clear intentions and visualizing your desires are essential parts of the manifestation process, they are only part of the equation. Manifestation is a dynamic partnership between intention and action. To bring your dreams to life, you must align your actions with your desires. This chapter delves into the importance of inspired action, teaches you how to recognize and seize opportunities aligned with your goals, and offers practical tips to maintain a high-energy focus throughout the day.

The Role of Inspired Action in Manifestation

The Law of Attraction works best when paired with inspired action—steps taken in alignment with your goals and guided by intuition or a sense of purpose. Inspired action is different from forced effort; it arises naturally, often accompanied by feelings of excitement, clarity, or curiosity. This type of action creates momentum and sends a strong signal to the universe that you are serious about your intentions.

Why Inspired Action Matters:

1. **It Bridges Intention and Reality:**
   Visualization and affirmations set the energetic blueprint, but action brings it into the physical world. By acting, you create tangible evidence of your commitment to your desires.

2. **It Builds Confidence and Momentum:**
   Each aligned step reinforces your belief in your ability to achieve your goals, creating a positive feedback loop that propels you forward.

3. **It Engages the Universe:**
   The universe responds to your willingness to move toward your goals by presenting new opportunities, resources, and synchronicities.

How to Identify Opportunities Aligned with Your Goals

Opportunities aligned with your desires often appear in subtle or unexpected ways. Recognizing and acting on them requires a combination of awareness, trust, and readiness.

1. Listen to Your Intuition

Your intuition is your internal compass, guiding you toward choices that resonate with your goals. Pay attention to gut feelings, hunches, or moments of inspiration—they are often clues from your subconscious or the universe.

Exercise to Strengthen Intuition:

- Take a few moments each day to sit quietly and ask yourself, "What's the next best step I can take toward my goal?"
- Listen without judgment and note any ideas or insights that arise.

2. Be Open to Synchronicities

Aligned opportunities often come disguised as coincidences or chance encounters. For example, a casual conversation might lead to a valuable connection or a book recommendation could contain the solution you need. Staying open and curious allows you to recognize these moments.

3. Evaluate Opportunities for Alignment

Not every opportunity that comes your way will be aligned with your goals. Before acting, ask yourself:

- Does this move me closer to my desired outcome?
- Does this feel exciting or energizing?
- Is this consistent with my values and vision?

If the answer is yes, take the next step. If not, trust that a better opportunity will come.

4. Take Small, Consistent Steps

Not all actions need to be grand or life-changing. Often, small, consistent steps build the momentum needed to manifest your goals. For example, if your goal is to write a book, committing to writing 200 words a day is an aligned action.

Tips for Maintaining High-Energy Focus Throughout the Day

High-energy focus is the foundation of productive, aligned action. By keeping your energy and mindset elevated, you can stay in alignment with your goals and take inspired actions effortlessly.

1. Start Your Day with Intention

How you begin your day sets the tone for everything that follows. Create a morning ritual that aligns your energy with your desires.

Morning Ritual Ideas:

- Spend five minutes visualizing your goals.
- Write down three specific actions you'll take that day to move closer to your dreams.
- Repeat affirmations like, "I am aligned with my highest good, and opportunities flow to me effortlessly."

2. Prioritize Self-Care

High-energy focus is impossible when you're running on empty. Prioritize activities that recharge you physically, mentally, and emotionally.

Self-Care Tips:

- Get enough sleep to stay mentally sharp.
- Stay hydrated and eat nourishing foods.
- Take breaks during the day to stretch, meditate, or simply breathe deeply.

3. Use Energy Anchors

Energy anchors are tools or practices that help you quickly shift back into alignment when you feel drained or distracted.

Examples of Energy Anchors:

- **Gratitude Practice:** Take 30 seconds to list three things you're grateful for.
- **Breathwork:** Inhale deeply for four counts, hold for four, and exhale for four. Repeat three times.
- **Movement:** A quick walk or stretching can refresh your body and mind.

4. Focus on One Task at a Time

Multitasking can dilute your energy and reduce the quality of your actions. Instead, commit fully to one task at a time, especially those aligned with your goals.

How to Stay Focused:

- Use a timer to dedicate blocks of uninterrupted time to important tasks.
- Eliminate distractions by silencing notifications or working in a clutter-free space.
- Set specific, achievable goals for each work session, such as "Finish drafting the first page of my proposal."

5. Celebrate Small Wins

Acknowledging your progress, no matter how small, reinforces your belief in your ability to manifest your desires.

Ways to Celebrate:

- Keep a journal of daily accomplishments and reflect on them each evening.
- Treat yourself to a small reward, like a favorite snack or a relaxing activity, when you complete an aligned action.
- Share your successes with a supportive friend or mentor.

Success Stories of Aligned Action

1. From Side Hustle to Business Owner:

Mia dreamed of starting her own graphic design business but wasn't sure how to begin. She decided to take small, aligned actions, such as creating a portfolio website and reaching out to one potential client each day. Within six months, she had replaced her day job income and was running her business full-time.

2. Manifesting a Dream Relationship:

Alex wanted to attract a loving partner. He began by aligning his actions with his goal, such as joining social activities that reflected his interests and practicing self-love. Through these steps, Alex met someone who shared his values and vision for the future.

3. Financial Breakthrough:

Sarah set a goal to save $10,000 in one year. She started by aligning her actions with her intention, creating a budget, and exploring freelance opportunities. Her inspired actions led to unexpected opportunities, including a high-paying project that allowed her to surpass her goal.

Conclusion

Aligning action with desire is the bridge between intention and manifestation. Inspired action, guided by intuition and fueled by focus, transforms dreams into reality. By identifying and acting on aligned opportunities and maintaining high-energy focus throughout your day, you strengthen the connection between your goals and the physical world. Remember, every step—no matter how small—is a declaration to the universe that you are ready to receive your desires. Trust the process, take inspired actions consistently, and watch your manifestations unfold.

Chapter 5: Trusting the Process and Letting Go

In the journey of manifestation, one of the most overlooked yet essential components is learning to trust the process and let go of attachment to the outcome. While taking inspired action and visualizing your desires are critical, clinging to them with desperation or doubt can create resistance and delay their realization. This chapter explores the role of trust and detachment in manifestation, introduces gratitude as a powerful tool for raising your vibration and maintaining faith, and provides methods for overcoming doubts and staying positive during challenging times.

The Role of Trust and Detachment in Manifestation

Manifestation is not solely about setting intentions and taking action; it also requires surrendering to the flow of the universe. Trusting the process involves believing that your desires are being fulfilled, even when you cannot see immediate evidence of progress. Detachment, on the other hand, means letting go of the need to control how or when your manifestations will arrive.

Why Trust and Detachment Are Crucial:

1. **Reduces Resistance:**
   Clinging to your desires with fear or impatience sends a signal of lack to the universe. Trust and detachment help you maintain an open, receptive energy that allows your goals to flow effortlessly into your life.

2. **Enhances Intuition:**
   When you release control, you become more attuned to intuitive nudges and synchronicities that guide you toward your desires.

3. **Preserves Emotional Well-Being:**
   Obsessing over outcomes can lead to stress, frustration, and burnout. Trust and detachment bring peace and joy to the manifestation process.

The Balance of Action and Trust:

Trusting the process does not mean being passive or indifferent. It means taking inspired action while releasing the need for constant validation or control. Think of it as planting a seed: you nurture it by watering and caring for it, but you trust nature to handle the growth.

Gratitude: A Tool for Raising Vibration and Maintaining Faith

Gratitude is one of the most powerful emotions for raising your vibration and fostering trust in the manifestation process. When you focus on what you already have, you shift your energy from lack to abundance, signaling to the universe that you are ready to receive more.

How Gratitude Enhances Manifestation:

1. **Amplifies Positive Energy:**
   Gratitude elevates your emotional state, aligning you with high-frequency vibrations that attract your desires.

2. **Reinforces Trust:**
   By appreciating the blessings already present in your life, you strengthen your belief in the universe's ability to provide.

3. **Reframes Challenges:**
   Gratitude helps you see obstacles as opportunities for growth and learning, keeping you optimistic even during setbacks.

Daily Gratitude Practices:

1. **Gratitude Journal:**
   Write down three to five things you are grateful for each day. Be specific and focus on both big and small blessings.
2. **Gratitude Visualization:**
   Spend a few minutes visualizing your desired outcome while expressing gratitude as if it has already manifested.
3. **Gratitude Affirmations:**
   Repeat affirmations like, "I am grateful for the abundance that flows into my life effortlessly."
4. **Gratitude Walks:**
   Take a walk and mentally note everything you appreciate around you, such as the beauty of nature or the kindness of others.

Overcoming Doubts and Staying Positive in Challenging Moments

Even the most seasoned manifestors face moments of doubt or challenges that test their faith. These moments are natural and can be transformed into opportunities for growth and deeper trust.

1. Reframe Doubts as Temporary Feelings

Doubt is a natural part of the human experience, but it doesn't have to derail your manifestation efforts. Instead of resisting doubt, acknowledge it and remind yourself that it is temporary and not reflective of the truth.

Steps to Reframe Doubts:

- Identify the specific thought or belief causing your doubt.
- Ask yourself: "Is this thought based on evidence or fear?"
- Replace the doubtful thought with an empowering affirmation. For example, replace "What if it doesn't work?" with "Everything is always working out for my highest good."

2. Use Mindfulness to Stay Present

Manifestation requires being in the present moment, where your energy and intentions are most powerful. Worrying about the future or dwelling on the past pulls your focus away from your goals.

Mindfulness Practices:

- **Deep Breathing:** Take slow, deep breaths to calm your mind and center yourself.
- **Body Scans:** Close your eyes and bring awareness to different parts of your body, releasing tension as you go.
- **Mindful Observation:** Focus on your surroundings, noticing colors, sounds, and textures without judgment.

3. Shift Focus with Positivity Boosters

When doubt creeps in, shift your energy by engaging in activities that uplift and inspire you.

Positivity Boosters:

- Listen to uplifting music or podcasts.
- Watch motivational videos or read success stories.
- Spend time with supportive friends or mentors who believe in your vision.
- Engage in hobbies or activities that bring you joy and relaxation.

4. Trust Through Affirmations and Mantras

Affirmations and mantras can help reinforce trust and calm your mind during uncertain times.

Examples of Affirmations for Trust:

- "I trust that the universe is always working in my favor."
- "I release all fear and embrace the flow of abundance."
- "My desires are on their way, and I am ready to receive them."

5. Focus on Progress, Not Perfection

Perfectionism can lead to unnecessary stress and self-doubt. Instead of fixating on the final outcome, celebrate the progress you've made along the way.

Steps to Focus on Progress:

- Keep a "progress log" to document your small wins and milestones.
- Reflect on how far you've come compared to where you started.
- Remind yourself that growth and learning are integral parts of the manifestation journey.

6. Surrender the How and When

One of the most common sources of doubt is obsessing over *how* and *when* your desires will manifest. Surrendering these details to the universe allows you to focus on the present and trust in divine timing.

Tips for Letting Go of the How and When:

- Replace "I need this to happen now" with "I trust this will happen at the perfect time."
- Create a symbolic ritual for surrender, such as writing your desires on paper and placing them in a "manifestation box" to release control.

Success Stories of Trust and Letting Go

1. A Dream Home Materialized:

Lucy visualized her dream home for months but felt frustrated when nothing seemed to happen. She decided to let go of her timeline, focus on gratitude, and trust the process. Shortly after, she discovered a listing for the perfect home within her budget—something she previously thought impossible.

2. A Career Opportunity Through Faith:

James wanted to switch careers but doubted his ability to succeed in a new field. Instead of giving in to fear, he focused on gratitude for his current job and trusted that the right opportunity would appear. Within weeks, a friend introduced him to someone hiring in his desired industry, leading to his dream job.

3. Healing and Peace After Letting Go:

Maria struggled with anxiety over a relationship issue. After practicing gratitude and using affirmations to trust the process, she released her need to control the outcome. As she shifted her energy, the relationship naturally healed, bringing both partners closer.

Conclusion

Trusting the process and letting go are vital elements of successful manifestation. When you release control and have faith in the universe, you create space for your desires to unfold in ways you may not have imagined. Gratitude is your anchor, keeping your energy high and your heart open, even during challenging times. By overcoming doubts and staying positive, you strengthen your connection to the universal flow, ensuring that your manifestations arrive at the perfect moment. Remember, the universe is always working behind the scenes to bring your dreams to life—your role is to trust, let go, and enjoy the journey.

Appendix A: 10 Quick Manifestation Exercises

Manifestation is a practice that thrives on consistency, focus, and the alignment of your thoughts and emotions with your desires. While the previous chapters have provided in-depth strategies for integrating manifestation into your daily life, this appendix offers a collection of ten quick, actionable exercises. These techniques are designed to accelerate your results by harnessing the power of scripting, vision boards, energy shifting, and more. Each exercise can be completed in just a few minutes, making them easy to incorporate into even the busiest schedules.

1. Scripting Your Desired Reality

Overview: Scripting involves writing a narrative of your life as if your desires have already manifested. This technique engages your imagination and emotions, aligning your subconscious mind with your goals.

Steps:

1. **Set Aside Time:** Allocate 5-10 minutes in a quiet space where you won't be disturbed.
2. **Choose a Focus:** Decide on a specific area of your life you want to manifest, such as career, relationships, or health.
3. **Write in the Present Tense:** Begin scripting your life as if your desires have already come true. Use vivid details and emotional language.
   - Example: "I am so grateful for my fulfilling job where I get to make a positive impact every day."
4. **Engage Your Senses:** Include descriptions that appeal to your senses—what you see, hear, feel, smell, and taste.
5. **Express Gratitude:** Throughout your script, express genuine gratitude for the manifestations.
6. **Read Aloud:** After writing, read your script aloud to reinforce the visualization.

Tips:

- Use a dedicated journal for your scripting exercises.
- Revisit and update your script regularly to keep it aligned with your evolving desires.

2. Creating a Vision Board

Overview: A vision board is a visual representation of your goals and desires. It serves as a daily reminder of what you're manifesting, helping to keep your focus and energy aligned.

Steps:

1. **Gather Materials:**
   - A poster board or corkboard
   - Magazines, printed images, quotes
   - Scissors, glue, pins, markers
2. **Define Your Goals:** Identify the specific goals you want to manifest.
3. **Select Images and Words:** Find pictures and words that represent your desires and resonate emotionally.
4. **Assemble Your Board:** Arrange and attach the images and words onto your board creatively.
5. **Place Your Board Prominently:** Put the vision board somewhere you'll see it daily, such as your bedroom or office.
6. **Visualize Daily:** Spend a few minutes each day looking at your board and imagining yourself experiencing those realities.

Tips:

- Digital Option: Create a digital vision board using apps or software if physical crafting isn't convenient.
- Keep it Updated: Refresh your vision board as your goals evolve or when you've manifested certain desires.

3. The 17-Second Focus Technique

Overview: Based on the idea that focusing on a thought for at least 17 seconds starts attracting similar thoughts and begins the manifestation process.

Steps:

1. **Choose a Specific Desire:** Pick one goal to focus on.
2. **Set a Timer:** Use a stopwatch or timer set for 17 seconds.
3. **Focus Intensely:** Close your eyes and concentrate solely on your desire, visualizing it vividly.
4. **Feel the Emotion:** Immerse yourself in the positive emotions associated with achieving your goal.
5. **Release Gently:** When the timer ends, take a deep breath and let go, trusting the process.

Tips:

- Extend to 68 Seconds: For a more powerful effect, repeat the 17-second focus four times consecutively.
- Consistency: Practice this technique multiple times a day to strengthen your manifestation power.

4. Energy Shifting with Music

Overview: Music can quickly alter your emotional state and raise your vibration, aligning you with the energy of your desires.

Steps:

1. **Create a Manifestation Playlist:** Compile songs that make you feel inspired, joyful, and aligned with your goals.
2. **Set Aside Time:** Take 5 minutes to listen to your playlist when you need an energy boost.
3. **Engage Fully:** As you listen, visualize your desires manifesting and feel the associated positive emotions.

4. **Move Your Body:** Dance, sway, or tap your feet to enhance the energy shift.

Tips:

- Use Headphones: To immerse yourself fully and minimize distractions.
- Update Regularly: Add new songs that resonate with your current goals and feelings.

5. Affirmation Cards

Overview: Affirmation cards are personalized statements that reinforce positive beliefs and intentions, aiding in reprogramming your subconscious mind.

Steps:

1. **Write Affirmations:** On small cards or sticky notes, write affirmations related to your desires.
     - Example: "I am attracting abundance in all areas of my life."
2. **Place Them Strategically:** Put the cards where you'll see them frequently—on mirrors, your desk, or in your wallet.
3. **Read Aloud Daily:** Whenever you see a card, pause to read the affirmation aloud with conviction.
4. **Feel the Words:** Internalize the affirmation by feeling the emotions it evokes.

Tips:

- Keep Them Positive: Phrase affirmations in a positive manner, focusing on what you want.
- Refresh Often: Update or rotate your affirmations to keep them meaningful and impactful.

6. Gratitude Rampage

Overview: A gratitude rampage involves rapidly listing things you're grateful for, shifting your focus to positivity and raising your vibration.

Steps:

1. **Set a Timer:** Allocate 2-3 minutes for this exercise.
2. **Begin Listing:** Either mentally or on paper, quickly list everything you're grateful for without overthinking.
3. **Include All Areas:** Mention small and big things—people, experiences, abilities, and possessions.
4. **Feel the Gratitude:** Allow yourself to genuinely feel thankful for each item you mention.
5. **Conclude with a Deep Breath:** Inhale deeply, exhale slowly, and carry this positive energy forward.

Tips:

- Do It Anytime: Especially effective when you're feeling down or unfocused.
- Expand Over Time: Aim to increase the duration or frequency as you become more attuned to gratitude.

7. Mirror Work

Overview: Mirror work involves speaking positive affirmations to yourself while looking in the mirror, enhancing self-love and belief in your manifestations.

Steps:

1. **Find Privacy:** Stand in front of a mirror where you can be alone.
2. **Make Eye Contact:** Look directly into your eyes to establish a connection.
3. **Speak Affirmations:** Say affirmations related to your desires aloud.

- Example: "I am confident and capable of achieving my dreams."

4. **Maintain Positive Body Language:** Stand tall, smile gently, and convey confidence.
5. **Repeat Daily:** Consistency strengthens the impact of this exercise.

Tips:

- Overcome Discomfort: It may feel awkward at first; persist to break through any resistance.
- Personalize Affirmations: Use words that resonate deeply with you.

8. The Two-Minute Journal

Overview: A brief journaling exercise to align your thoughts and emotions with your goals, promoting clarity and focus.

Steps:

1. **Set a Timer:** Allocate two minutes for focused journaling.
2. **Choose a Prompt:** Use prompts like:
    - "What do I want to manifest today?"
    - "How will I feel when I achieve my goal?"
3. **Write Freely:** Without worrying about grammar or structure, write whatever comes to mind.
4. **Reflect Briefly:** After writing, read over your words and absorb their meaning.

Tips:

- Keep It Handy: Use a small notebook or digital app for convenience.

- Morning or Night: Practice at the start or end of your day to set intentions or reflect.

9. Breathing Visualization

Overview: Combining deep breathing with visualization to quickly center yourself and align with your desires.

Steps:

1. **Find a Comfortable Position:** Sit or stand with a straight spine.
2. **Close Your Eyes:** Begin taking slow, deep breaths.
3. **Visualize on Inhale:** As you inhale, imagine breathing in light, success, or abundance.
4. **Release on Exhale:** As you exhale, imagine releasing doubt, fear, or negativity.
5. **Focus on Your Desire:** On each inhale, visualize your goal manifesting.
6. **Repeat for 5 Breaths:** This takes approximately one minute but can be extended as desired.

Tips:

- Use Anytime: Particularly useful before important meetings or decisions.
- Enhance with Affirmations: Mentally recite affirmations in sync with your breaths.

10. Random Acts of Kindness

Overview: Performing acts of kindness raises your vibration and attracts positive energy, indirectly supporting your manifestation efforts.

Steps:

1. **Identify Opportunities:** Look for simple ways to help others throughout your day.
   - Examples: Holding the door open, complimenting a stranger, or helping a coworker.
2. **Act Selflessly:** Perform the act without expecting anything in return.
3. **Feel the Joy:** Allow the positive emotions from your kindness to elevate your mood.
4. **Reflect Briefly:** Acknowledge how these actions align you with abundance and positivity.

Tips:

- Make It a Habit: Incorporate kindness into your daily routine.
- Be Genuine: Choose actions that you feel authentically compelled to perform.

Final Thoughts

These ten quick manifestation exercises are tools to enhance your journey toward realizing your desires. They are designed to be flexible and adaptable to your lifestyle, ensuring that you can maintain a high vibrational state and focused intention no matter how busy you are. Remember, the key to manifestation is not just the actions themselves but the consistency and emotion behind them. By integrating these practices into your daily routine, you accelerate your ability to attract and receive the abundance you seek.

Experiment with different exercises to discover which resonate most with you, and don't hesitate to combine them for greater impact. Your manifestation journey is a personal and evolving process—embrace it with openness, joy, and confidence.

Appendix B: Resources for Mastering the Law of Attraction

Mastering the Law of Attraction is a lifelong journey of learning, practice, and refinement. The more you immerse yourself in its principles and techniques, the more confident and adept you'll become at manifesting your desires. This appendix provides a curated list of recommended books, apps, and online communities to deepen your understanding and enhance your practice. Additionally, it includes a manifestation tracker template to help you monitor your progress, reflect on your journey, and celebrate your wins.

Recommended Books

The following books are foundational resources for understanding and applying the Law of Attraction. They cover a range of perspectives, from philosophical insights to practical techniques:

1. **"The Secret" by Rhonda Byrne**
   - A classic introduction to the Law of Attraction, exploring how thoughts and emotions shape reality. Ideal for beginners.
2. **"Ask and It Is Given" by Esther and Jerry Hicks**
   - A deep dive into the teachings of Abraham, providing 22 practical processes to align your energy with your desires.
3. **"The Power of Now" by Eckhart Tolle**
   - While not solely focused on the Law of Attraction, this book emphasizes the importance of mindfulness and presence in creating your ideal reality.
4. **"Think and Grow Rich" by Napoleon Hill**
   - A timeless guide to achieving success through focused thought, visualization, and persistent action.
5. **"You Are a Badass at Making Money" by Jen Sincero**
   - A motivational and humorous take on using the Law of Attraction to manifest financial abundance.

6. **"Creative Visualization" by Shakti Gawain**
   - A comprehensive guide to visualization techniques, offering practical exercises and examples.
7. **"The Alchemist" by Paulo Coelho**
   - A fictional story filled with profound insights about following your dreams and trusting the process.

Recommended Apps

Technology can make it easier to stay consistent with your manifestation practice. These apps provide tools and reminders to keep you focused and aligned with your goals:

1. **ThinkUp**
   - Create and record personalized affirmations to listen to daily. Ideal for reprogramming your subconscious mind.
2. **Vision Board**
   - A digital vision board app that lets you create and update visual representations of your goals on your phone or tablet.
3. **Grateful: A Gratitude Journal**
   - A simple yet powerful tool to record and reflect on what you're grateful for, helping to raise your vibration.
4. **Law of Attraction Toolbox**
   - Offers guided exercises, meditations, and manifestation games based on Abraham-Hicks teachings.
5. **Calm or Insight Timer**
   - Meditation apps with specific sessions focused on visualization, mindfulness, and raising vibration.
6. **Trello or Notion**
   - Use these productivity apps to create manifestation trackers, organize your goals, and log your progress.

Online Communities

Joining a community of like-minded individuals can provide encouragement, share insights, and keep you motivated:

1. **Reddit: r/LawofAttraction**
   - A vibrant online community where members share success stories, tips, and answer questions about the Law of Attraction.
2. **Facebook Groups:**
   - Look for groups like "Manifestation Nation" or "The Secret Official Community" to connect with others on similar journeys.
3. **Meetup**
   - Search for local Law of Attraction or personal development groups to meet people in person and attend workshops.
4. **Mindvalley Tribe**
   - An online learning platform with a community of individuals focused on personal growth and manifestation practices.
5. **Instagram and TikTok:**
   - Follow accounts that share daily affirmations, tips, and motivational content. Popular hashtags like #LawOfAttraction and #Manifestation can help you find valuable content.

Manifestation Tracker Template

Tracking your manifestation progress is a powerful way to stay focused, measure results, and celebrate your wins. Use this template to document your journey and refine your practice:

Manifestation Tracker Template

Date	Desire/Goal	Actions Taken	Emotions Experienced	Signs Ex-/Synchronicities	Outcome/ Progress	Gratitude Reflection
MM /DD/ YYYY	Write your specific goal or desire.	List the steps or actions you took to align with your goal (e.g., visualization, scripting, inspired actions).	Record how you felt while working toward your goal (e.g., excited, confident, doubtful).	Note any signs, synchronicities, or coincidences you noticed (e.g., angel numbers, unexpected opportunities).	Describe any progress or outcomes (e.g., a job offer, meeting the right person, receiving clarity).	Reflect on what you're grateful for in this process (e.g., lessons learned, progress made).

How to Use the Tracker

1. **Daily or Weekly Entries:**
   Set aside time each day or week to fill out the tracker.
2. **Look for Patterns:**
   Review your entries regularly to identify patterns or areas where you can adjust your approach.
3. **Celebrate Wins:**
   Use the "Gratitude Reflection" section to appreciate every step of your journey, even if the ultimate goal hasn't yet manifested.

Final Thoughts

The resources and tools in this appendix are designed to deepen your understanding of the Law of Attraction and make your manifestation practice more structured and effective. Whether you immerse yourself in inspiring books, engage with supportive communities, or use the tracker to monitor your journey, these methods will keep you motivated and aligned. Remember, manifestation is a personal journey, and the right tools can help you stay connected to your desires while enjoying the process. Stay consistent, trust the universe, and celebrate every step toward creating the life you envision.

<u>Message from the Author:</u>

I hope you enjoyed this book, I love astrology and knew there was not a book such as this out on the shelf. I love metaphysical items as well. Please check out my other books:

-Life of Government Benefits

-My life of Hell

-My life with Hydrocephalus

-Red Sky

-World Domination:Woman's rule

-World Domination:Woman's Rule 2: The War

-Life and Banishment of Apophis: book 1

-The Kidney Friendly Diet

-The Ultimate Hemp Cookbook

-Creating a Dispensary(legally)

-Cleanliness throughout life: the importance of showering from childhood to adulthood.

-Strong Roots: The Risks of Overcoddling children

-Hemp Horoscopes: Cosmic Insights and Earthly Healing

- Celestial Hemp Navigating the Zodiac: Through the Green Cosmos

-Astrological Hemp: Aligning The Stars with Earth's Ancient Herb

-The Astrological Guide to Hemp: Stars, Signs, and Sacred Leaves

-Green Growth: Innovative Marketing Strategies for your Hemp Products and Dispensary

-Cosmic Cannabis

-Astrological Munchies

-Henry The Hemp

-Zodiacal Roots: The Astrological Soul Of Hemp

- **Green Constellations: Intersection of Hemp and Zodiac**
-Hemp in The Houses: An astrological Adventure Through The Cannabis Galaxy
-Galactic Ganja Guide
Heavenly Hemp
Zodiac Leaves
Doctor Who Astrology
Cannastrology
Stellar Satvias and Cosmic Indicas
<u>Celestial Cannabis: A Zodiac Journey</u>
AstroHerbology: The Sky and The Soil: Volume 1
AstroHerbology:Celestial Cannabis:Volume 2
Cosmic Cannabis Cultivation
The Starry Guide to Herbal Harmony: Volume 1
The Starry Guide to Herbal Harmony: Cannabis Universe: Volume 2
Yugioh Astrology: Astrological Guide to Deck, Duels and more
Nightmare Mansion: Echoes of The Abyss
Nightmare Mansion 2: Legacy of Shadows
Nightmare Mansion 3: Shadows of the Forgotten
Nightmare Mansion 4: Echoes of the Damned
The Life and Banishment of Apophis: Book 2
Nightmare Mansion: Halls of Despair
<u>Healing with Herb: Cannabis and Hydrocephalus</u>
<u>Planetary Pot: Aligning with Astrological Herbs: Volume 1</u>
Fast Track to Freedom: 30 Days to Financial Independence Using AI, Assets, and Agile Hustles
<u>Cosmic Hemp Pathways</u>
How to Become Financially Free in 30 Days: 10,000 Paths to Prosperity
Zodiacal Herbage: Astrological Insights: Volume 1
Nightmare Mansion: Whispers in the Walls
The Daleks Invade Atlantis

Henry the hemp and Hydrocephalus

10X The Kidney Friendly Diet

Cannabis Universe: Adult coloring book

Hemp Astrology: The Healing Power of the Stars

Zodiacal Herbage: Astrological Insights: Cannabis Universe: Volume 2

<u>**Planetary Pot: Aligning with Astrological Herbs: Cannabis Universes: Volume 2**</u>

Doctor Who Meets the Replicators and SG-1: The Ultimate Battle for Survival

Nightmare Mansion: Curse of the Blood Moon

<u>**The Celestial Stoner: A Guide to the Zodiac**</u>

Cosmic Pleasures: Sex Toy Astrology for Every Sign

Hydrocephalus Astrology: Navigating the Stars and Healing Waters

Lapis and the Mischievous Chocolate Bar

Celestial Positions: Sexual Astrology for Every Sign

Apophis's Shadow Work Journal: : A Journey of Self-Discovery and Healing

Kinky Cosmos: Sexual Kink Astrology for Every Sign

Digital Cosmos: The Astrological Digimon Compendium

Stellar Seeds: The Cosmic Guide to Growing with Astrology

Apophis's Daily Gratitude Journal

Cat Astrology: Feline Mysteries of the Cosmos

The Cosmic Kama Sutra: An Astrological Guide to Sexual Positions

Unleash Your Potential: A Guided Journal Powered by AI Insights

Whispers of the Enchanted Grove

Cosmic Pleasures: An Astrological Guide to Sexual Kinks

369, 12 Manifestation Journal

Whisper of the nocturne journal(blank journal for writing or drawing)

The Boogey Book

Locked In Reflection: A Chastity Journey Through Locktober

Generating Wealth Quickly:

How to Generate $100,000 in 24 Hours

Star Magic: Harness the Power of the Universe

The Flatulence Chronicles: A Fart Journal for Self-Discovery

The Doctor and The Death Moth

Seize the Day: A Personal Seizure Tracking Journal

The Ultimate Boogeyman Safari: A Journey into the Boogie World and Beyond

Whispers of Samhain: 1,000 Spells of Love, Luck, and Lunar Magic: Samhain Spell Book

Apophis's guides:

Witch's Spellbook Crafting Guide for Halloween

<u>Frost & Flame: The Enchanted Yule Grimoire of 1000 Winter Spells</u>

<u>The Ultimate Boogey Goo Guide & Spooky Activities for Halloween Fun</u>

Harmony of the Scales: A Libra's Spellcraft for Balance and Beauty

The Enchanted Advent: 36 Days of Christmas Wonders

Nightmare Mansion: The Labyrinth of Screams

Harvest of Enchantment: 1,000 Spells of Gratitude, Love, and Fortune for Thanksgiving

The Boogey Chronicles: A Journal of Nightly Encounters and Shadowy Secrets

The 12 Days of Financial Freedom: A Step-by-Step Christmas Countdown to Transform Your Finances

Sigil of the Eternal Spiral Blank Journal

A Christmas Feast: Timeless Recipes for Every Meal

Holiday Stress-Free Solutions: A Survival Guide to Thriving During the Festive Season

Yu-Gi-Oh! Holiday Gifting Mastery: The Ultimate Guide for Fans and Newcomers Alike

Holiday Harmony: A Hydrocephalus Survival Guide for the Festive Season

Celestial Craft: The Witch's Almanac for 2025 – A Cosmic Guide to Manifestations, Moons, and Mystical Events

Doctor Who: The Toymaker's Winter Wonderland

Tulsa King Unveiled: A Thrilling Guide to Stallone's Mafia Masterpiece

Pendulum Craft: A Complete Guide to Crafting and Using Personalized Divination Tools

Nightmare Mansion: Santa's Eternal Eve

Starlight Noel: A Cosmic Journey through Christmas Mysteries

The Dark Architect: Unlocking the Blueprint of Existence

Surviving the Embrace: The Ultimate Guide to Encounters with The Hugging Molly

The Enchanted Codex: Secrets of the Craft for Witches, Wiccans, and Pagans

Harvest of Gratitude: A Complete Thanksgiving Guide

Yuletide Essentials: A Complete Guide to an Authentic and Magical Christmas

Celestial Smokes: A Cosmic Guide to Cigars and Astrology

Living in Balance: A Comprehensive Survival Guide to Thriving with Diabetes Insipidus

Cosmic Symbiosis: The Venom Zodiac Chronicles

The Cursed Paw of Ambition

Cosmic Symbiosis: The Astrological Venom Journal

Celestial Wonders Unfold: A Stargazer's Guide to the Cosmos (2024-2029)

The Ultimate Black Friday Prepper's Guide: Mastering Shopping Strategies and Savings

Cosmic Sales: The Astrological Guide to Black Friday Shopping

Legends of the Corn Mother and Other Harvest Myths

Whispers of the Harvest: The Corn Mother's Journal

The Evergreen Spellbook

The Doctor Meets the Boogeyman

The White Witch of Rose Hall's SpellBook

The Gingerbread Golem's Shadow: A Study in Sweet Darkness

The Gingerbread Golem Codex: An Academic Exploration of Sweet Myths

The Gingerbread Golem Grimoire: Sweet Magicks and Spells for the Festive Witch

The Curse of the Gingerbread Golem

10-minute Christmas Crafts for kids

<u>Christmas Crisis Solutions: The Ultimate Last-Minute Survival Guide</u>

Gingerbread Golem Recipes: Holiday Treats with a Magical Twist

The Infinite Key: Unlocking Mystical Secrets of the Ages

Enchanted Yule: A Wiccan and Pagan Guide to a Magical and Memorable Season

Dinosaurs of Power: Unlocking Ancient Magick

Astro-Dinos: The Cosmic Guide to Prehistoric Wisdom

Gallifrey's Yule Logs: A Festive Doctor Who Cookbook

The Dino Grimoire: Secrets of Prehistoric Magick

The Gift They Never Knew They Needed

The Gingerbread Golem's Culinary Alchemy: Enchanting Recipes for a Sweetly Dark Feast

A Time Lord Christmas: Holiday Adventures with the Doctor

Krampusproofing Your Home: Defensive Strategies for Yule

Silent Frights: A Collection of Christmas Creepypastas to Chill Your Bones

Santa Raptor's Jolly Carnage: A Dino-Claus Christmas Tale

Prehistoric Palettes: A Dino Wicca Coloring Journey
The Christmas Wishkeeper Chronicles
The Starlight Sleigh: A Holiday Journey
Elf Secrets: The True Magic of the North Pole
Candy Cane Conjurations
Cooking with Kids: Recipes Under 20 Minutes
Doctor Who: The TARDIS Confiscation
The Anxiety First Aid Kit: Quick Tools to Calm Your Mind
Frosty Whispers: A Winter's Tale
The Infinite Key: Unlocking the Secrets to Prosperity, Resilience, and Purpose
The Grasping Void: Why You'll Regret This Purchase
Astrology for Busy Bees: Star Signs Simplified
The Instant Focus Formula: Cut Through the Noise
The Secret Language of Colors: Unlocking the Emotional Codes
Sacred Fossil Chronicles: Blank Journal
The Christmas Cottage Miracle
Feeding Frenzy: Graboid-Inspired Recipes

If you want solar for your home go here: https://www.harborsolar.live/apophisenterprises/

Get Some Tarot cards: https://www.makeplayingcards.com/sell/apophis-occult-shop

Get some shirts: https://www.bonfire.com/store/apophis-shirt-emporium/

<u>**Instagrams:**</u>
@apophis_enterprises,
@apophisbookemporium,
@apophisscardshop
Twitter: @apophisenterpr1
 Tiktok:@apophisenterprise
Youtube: @sg1fan23477, @FiresideRetreatKingdom
Hive: @sg1fan23477
CheeLee: @SG1fan23477

Podcast: Apophis Chat Zone: https://open.spotify.com/show/5zXbrCLEV2xzCp8ybrfHsk?si=fb4d4fdbdce44dec

Newsletter: https://apophiss-newsletter-27c897.beehiiv.com/

If you want to support me or see posts of other projects that I have come over to: **buymeacoffee.com/mpetchinskg**
I post there daily several times a day

Get your Dinowicca or Christmas themed digital products, especially Santa Raptor songs and other musics. Here: **https://sg1fan23477.gumroad.com**

Apophis Yuletide Digital has not only digital Christmas items, but it will have all things with Dinowicca as well as other Digital products.

www.ingramcontent.com/pod-product-compliance
Lightning Source LLC
Chambersburg PA
CBHW072123150726
47999CB00005B/2109